Create a
Mobile App from Scratch

Build and Launch Your First App in 30 Days – No Programming Experience Required

Aaron Lynas

Disclaimer

The information and instructions provided in this book are intended for general guidance and educational purposes only. The author and publisher make no representations or warranties regarding the accuracy or completeness of the content, and any actions taken based on the information in this book are done at the reader's own risk.

While every effort has been made to ensure the safety and effectiveness of the projects presented, the author and publisher are not liable for any injury, loss, or damage that may occur from the use of materials, tools, or techniques described in this book. Readers are encouraged to exercise caution and follow all relevant safety guidelines and manufacturer instructions when undertaking any of the projects.

By using the information provided, you acknowledge and accept these terms.

TABLE OF CONTENTS

INTRODUCTION

In a world where smartphones are practically an extension of ourselves, mobile apps have become the gateway to innovation, connection, and problem-solving. Every day, new ideas transform into powerful tools in the palms of millions. Yet, for many aspiring creators, the path to building an app seems blocked by a formidable wall: the need to code.

This book is here to tell you that wall no longer exists.

Welcome to a new era—where building a mobile app doesn't require a computer science degree, years of technical training, or even a single line of code. Whether you're an entrepreneur with a business idea, a creative thinker looking to bring a concept to life, or someone who simply loves learning new things, *Create a Mobile App from Scratch* is your step-by-step guide to turning your vision into a working product—fast, affordably, and without prior experience.

Over the next ten chapters, you'll learn how to shape your idea into a well-designed app using the power of intuitive no-code platforms. You'll discover how to plan, design, build, test, and launch an app within 30 days—even if you've never opened a programming book in your life. More importantly, you'll gain the confidence that you *can* create something valuable with the tools now at your fingertips.

This is not just a book about app creation. It's a guide to empowerment. A blueprint for turning ideas into action. And most of all, a reminder that the only thing standing between you and your first app—is the decision to start.

Let's begin.

CHAPTER ONE
From Idea to Vision – The Birth of Your App

The journey of creating a mobile app does not begin with lines of code or visual design—it begins with an idea. But not just any idea. It begins with an idea that solves a real-world problem, meets a genuine need, or enhances the way people interact with the world. Chapter One lays the foundation for your entire mobile app project.

Before diving into platforms, designs, and features, you need clarity: what is your app truly about, who is it for, and what problem does it solve? This chapter explores how to identify a compelling idea, how to validate it through market research, and how to define your target audience—the three pillars of a successful mobile app concept.

1.1 Finding Your Big Idea: How to Spot a Real Problem and Brainstorm Your App's Purpose

Many aspiring app creators begin with a vague desire to build "something useful" or "something popular," but they often struggle to translate that impulse into a concrete concept. The truth is, great apps don't start with technology; they start with people. Specifically, they start with a problem people face—something frustrating, inefficient, outdated, or just missing entirely.

To uncover your big idea, look around you. Pay attention to everyday annoyances in your personal or professional life. Is there a daily task that feels overly complicated? A common situation where people are constantly improvising a solution? A missed opportunity for connection or efficiency? Every inconvenience is a potential goldmine for innovation.

For instance, the idea behind Uber didn't begin as a transportation platform—it began as two friends in Paris frustrated by the difficulty of hailing a cab in the rain. Their solution evolved into a global service that reshaped how the world moves.

Another strategy is to think about your own interests, hobbies, or communities you belong to. Perhaps you are a fitness enthusiast and notice that most fitness tracking apps lack a certain feature, like personalized encouragement or integration with niche workouts.

Or maybe you're a teacher who sees the daily struggle of students staying organized with assignments. Tapping into your lived experience gives you an edge because you already understand the environment and challenges of your potential users.

Once you've identified a problem or area for improvement, begin brainstorming potential ways an app could solve it. Don't worry at this stage about technical limitations or feasibility—just focus on the user need.

Imagine what the ideal experience would look like. How could your app save time, reduce frustration, or create joy? What would be the simplest, clearest path for a user to reach their goal using your solution?

Your big idea should sit at the intersection of three important elements: a real-world problem, a feasible mobile solution, and a purpose that excites you. If your idea checks those boxes, you've found the seed from which a successful app can grow.

1.2 Researching the Market: Validate Your Idea by Exploring Similar Apps and Gaps

Once your app idea has taken shape, the next critical step is to validate it. Market validation is about confirming that your idea has potential—before investing time and energy into development. This process involves identifying existing solutions, understanding the competitive landscape, and spotting opportunities where your app can stand out.

Begin by searching the app stores—both Apple's App Store and Google Play—for apps that resemble your idea. Use keywords related to the function of your app and explore what's currently available.

Download the top-rated options and analyze them carefully. What do they do well? Where do they fall short? Are there patterns in user reviews that hint at unmet needs? These reviews often contain hidden gems: complaints about confusing interfaces, feature requests, or desires for customization. Take notes on everything you discover.

This research serves two purposes. First, it shows that there is already demand for your type of app, which is a good sign. Contrary to popular belief, having competitors is not a bad thing—it means there's a market. Second, it helps you identify your differentiator: the unique angle your app can take to do something better, faster, easier, or more affordably.

Let's say you're building a meal-planning app. A quick survey of existing apps might show you that while many apps offer recipes, few cater to specific dietary needs like low-FODMAP, or support users who cook on a tight budget. That's your opening. Your app can serve the same general need but provide a unique experience tailored to a specific niche.

Additionally, look beyond the app stores. Visit forums, Reddit threads, Facebook groups, and Quora discussions related to your topic. What are people talking about? What frustrations do they voice? Are there workarounds or homegrown solutions that people rely on because no good app exists yet?

Once you've gathered this information, write a brief analysis of your competitive landscape. Highlight the strengths and weaknesses of existing apps, describe how your app will be different, and articulate what unique value you bring to the user. This exercise will not only clarify your vision but also give you a strong foundation when it's time to pitch your app to potential users, collaborators, or even investors.

In the validation process, remember: it's not about having an idea no one has ever had before—it's about solving a problem in a way that's meaningfully better than what's currently available.

1.3 Defining Your Target User: Identify Your Ideal Audience and What They Truly Need

Even the most innovative app idea will fall flat if it doesn't resonate with the right audience. That's why defining your target user is one of the most essential steps in the early stages of app development. This process isn't about excluding people—it's about knowing who you're designing for, so every decision you make is rooted in empathy and relevance.

Start by imagining your ideal user. Be as specific as possible. Are they students, parents, freelancers, small business owners, or retirees? How old are they? What devices do they use most? What does a day in their life look like? The more detailed your profile, the better. This "user persona" helps you visualize not just who your app is for, but how they might discover, use, and benefit from it.

Let's say your app idea is focused on helping busy professionals manage their wellness routines. Your ideal user might be a 35-year-old corporate employee who works long hours, struggles to maintain a healthy lifestyle, and uses their smartphone for time management.

Understanding this context helps you prioritize features—perhaps your app should include short, 5-minute guided workouts, quick meal suggestions, and daily reminders instead of long tutorials or elaborate setups.

To gather real insights, you can interview people who resemble your target user. Ask open-ended questions about their habits, frustrations, and desires. Pay close attention to how they describe their pain points.

You're not just looking for what they say they want—you're listening for what they *need*. Sometimes users can't articulate the perfect solution, but their experiences offer clues. If several people express that they forget to drink water throughout the day, your app might include a gentle hydration reminder as a small but valuable feature.

Don't try to serve everyone. A generic app for "everyone" ends up appealing to no one. Instead, focus your energy on delighting a specific group with precision. Once your app gains traction and loyalty within that niche, you can always expand features or widen your audience later.

Another important consideration is the emotional aspect of your app. How do you want your users to feel when they use it? Empowered? Relaxed? Organized? Inspired? These emotional responses shape not only the features but also the tone, branding, and design of your app. By understanding both the practical and emotional needs of your target user, you create something that doesn't just function—it connects.

CHAPTER TWO
Planning Like a Pro – Setting a Strong Foundation

Every successful app is built on a solid foundation— one rooted not in flashy features or cutting-edge technology, but in clarity, focus, and intentional design. While it might be tempting to rush into development after landing on your big idea, it is the planning phase that separates apps that flourish from those that fade into obscurity.

This chapter walks you through the essential first steps in building your app's blueprint: identifying the right features to prioritize, mapping out your user's journey, and crafting a lean, functional Minimum Viable Product (MVP). These strategies are especially vital when working within limited resources or without programming experience, as they ensure that every hour you invest is purposeful and directed toward your goal.

2.1 Outlining Core Features: Choose the Most Important Features to Build First

With your app idea validated and your target audience defined, it's time to zoom in on the actual features your app will offer. One of the most common mistakes made by first-time app creators is trying to do too much, too soon. It's easy to fall into the trap of adding every conceivable feature in the hope of creating something comprehensive. But successful apps are not built by offering everything—they are built by doing a few things exceptionally well.

Begin by returning to the problem your app is solving. Ask yourself: what is the *one key action* users must be able to complete for the app to be useful? That's your core feature. For a to-do list app, it might be adding and organizing tasks. For a meal planner, it could be generating weekly menus based on dietary preferences. This central functionality should be the first and most important element you plan around.

Once you've identified the core feature, brainstorm supporting features that enhance the experience but aren't absolutely essential. These might include social sharing options, customizable settings, or bonus content. These can be added later—what matters now is focusing on the foundation. Think of your app like a house: you start with the framework and structure, not the wallpaper and decorations.

To help organize your thoughts, create a simple list divided into three categories: **Must-Have**, **Nice-to-Have**, and **Future Features**. This approach allows you to stay lean and focused without discarding your longer-term vision. Each feature you include should have a clear justification: Does it solve a problem? Does it simplify the user's experience? Does it bring the user closer to their goal?

Also, consider how each feature fits into the overall user experience. Too many options early on can overwhelm users. Streamlining your feature set ensures a faster, more intuitive experience—crucial for encouraging first-time users to return. When in doubt, remember that simplicity is powerful. Many of the world's most-used apps started with just one or two core features and gradually evolved based on user feedback and usage data.

Your job during this stage is to define what your app *must do* to deliver value from day one. Focus on usability, functionality, and user satisfaction—not complexity.

2.2 Sketching User Flows: Map Out What Your User Will See and Do Step by Step

Now that you've identified your app's core features, it's time to map out how users will interact with them. This process—called sketching user flows— helps you visualize the sequence of actions a user will take within your app. It's like drawing a map before a journey: you might not know every detail of the terrain yet, but you need to chart the key paths and turning points.

A user flow is essentially a step-by-step diagram that outlines how a user gets from one point to another.

For example, if your app's core function is booking fitness classes, a basic user flow might look like this: **Open App → View Classes → Select Class → Book Class → Receive Confirmation**. Each step represents a screen or interaction, helping you break down complex processes into manageable components.

Sketching these flows doesn't require any fancy tools or design experience. You can start with pen and paper, whiteboards, or free digital wireframing tools like Figma, Balsamiq, or Whimsical. The key is to focus on logic and clarity, not visual polish. Your goal is to understand what the user sees, what actions they can take, and how the app responds.

Start by identifying your primary user goals. What are the main actions you want users to complete in your app? Then, ask yourself what needs to happen before, during, and after each action. What decisions must the user make? What information must they input? What confirmations or feedback will they receive?

Pay special attention to *entry points* and *exit points* in your app. Entry points are how users arrive at a particular feature or screen, while exit points are where they leave or move to another part of the app. These transitions should feel seamless. For instance, after a user books a class, they might want to share it on social media or add it to their calendar—both of which are logical next steps.

As you sketch, keep the user's experience at the forefront. Avoid dead ends, confusing loops, or unnecessary steps. Imagine the user is a guest in your digital home—your job is to make their visit welcoming, intuitive, and productive.

One powerful way to test your user flow early is to walk through it yourself or with others using simple paper prototypes. Ask a friend or colleague to perform a task using your sketch, and observe where they hesitate, get confused, or ask questions. These insights are invaluable and allow you to refine your plan before development begins.

A clear, efficient user flow ensures your app feels logical and enjoyable from the moment someone opens it. It forms the basis of your app's layout and navigation—two areas where great planning pays massive dividends later.

2.3 Creating a Simple MVP Plan: Learn the Concept of a Minimum Viable Product (MVP) and Keep It Lean

With your features outlined and user flows mapped, you're now ready to develop a strategic roadmap: your Minimum Viable Product (MVP). The MVP is a stripped-down version of your app that includes only the features necessary to satisfy early users and prove the value of your idea. Think of it as your app's "Version 1.0"—the lean, functional version that gets you into the market quickly.

The concept of an MVP originated in the world of startups but applies just as powerfully to app development. Rather than spending months or years building a complex app with every imaginable feature, the MVP approach allows you to launch faster, gather feedback, and evolve based on real-world usage. It's efficient, user-centered, and especially effective for solo creators or small teams.

Start your MVP planning by reviewing your "Must-Have" feature list from earlier. What is the single most valuable function your app must perform for it to be useful? That is the core of your MVP. Add only the features that directly support or enable this core function. Everything else—no matter how exciting or ambitious—can be scheduled for a future release.

Your MVP should also be technically feasible using no-code or low-code platforms, which allow you to build interactive apps without writing software from scratch. These tools include platforms like Adalo, Glide, Bubble, or Thunkable, which are powerful enough to support most MVPs. Their drag-and-drop interfaces, prebuilt components, and logic-based workflows make them perfect for first-time builders.

Don't let perfectionism slow you down. The purpose of your MVP is not to dazzle users with a finished product, but to test assumptions, gather data, and prove that people are willing to use your app. You'll learn more in a week of real user feedback than in months of hypothetical planning.

To ensure your MVP stays lean, establish clear launch criteria. What does "ready to launch" mean for you? It could be when users can register, use the main feature, and complete a single successful interaction. Document your MVP goals and timelines, and stick to them. Overbuilding delays your ability to validate your app and can waste time on features that users might not even want.

After launch, treat your MVP as a living project. Monitor user behavior, ask for feedback, and make data-driven decisions about what to build next. In many cases, your users will surprise you—they may use your app in unexpected ways or request features you hadn't considered. This iterative, responsive approach is far more effective than guessing what people want from the start.

CHAPTER THREE
Design Without Code – Bringing Your App to Life Visually

Design is where your app truly begins to take form in the eyes of users. It's the bridge between your ideas and your users' experiences, translating functionality into form. While it's easy to think of design as merely "making things look nice," effective app design goes much deeper. It communicates your app's purpose, builds user trust, and influences behavior.

The beauty of today's no-code movement is that you no longer need to be a trained graphic designer or developer to craft a stunning user interface. With a clear understanding of mobile design principles, the right tools, and a thoughtful approach to aesthetics, anyone can shape a compelling visual identity for their app.

This chapter will guide you step by step through the process of designing your app without writing a single line of code—from learning the fundamentals of mobile design, to wireframing your app's structure, to selecting a design style that aligns with your brand and users.

3.1 Principles of Good Mobile Design: Understand Layout, Color, and Usability Basics

Good mobile design is more than attractive visuals. It's a strategic approach to organizing content and functionality in a way that feels natural, intuitive, and delightful. When design is done right, users don't even notice it—it simply works. When it's done poorly, even the most innovative features can become frustrating and unusable.

One of the foundational principles of effective mobile design is **clarity**. On a small screen, space is limited. Every element must serve a purpose. Cluttered layouts confuse users and obscure functionality. Instead, embrace simplicity. Make buttons large enough to tap with ease. Place the most important features front and center, avoiding excessive menus and options that overwhelm users.

Next, consider **hierarchy**. This refers to the visual order of elements on a screen. You want users to know instinctively where to look and what to do next. Larger text, bolder colors, and strategic placement help guide users' eyes.

Headlines should be prominent, while secondary content should be visually subdued. Think about how users will scan the screen: typically, from top to bottom and left to right (in most Western languages). Use this flow to your advantage by positioning key calls-to-action where they're likely to be seen.

Color is another powerful tool in the designer's toolkit. It's not just about looking appealing—it's about conveying meaning and emotion. Warm colors like red and orange evoke energy and urgency, while cool tones like blue and green feel calming and trustworthy. Be consistent with your color choices. Use a primary color for interactive elements (such as buttons and icons), and support it with a complementary palette for backgrounds and text. Always ensure readability by maintaining strong contrast between text and background colors.

Typography also plays a crucial role. Use no more than two or three fonts in your app design to maintain a cohesive look. Choose fonts that are legible at small sizes, and be mindful of how they appear on different screen resolutions. Avoid using all caps for long paragraphs, and ensure text elements are properly aligned and spaced for ease of reading.

Finally, **usability** is paramount. Your design must cater to the user's needs, not your personal preferences. Include intuitive navigation—such as back buttons, menus, and tab bars—that helps users move smoothly from one screen to another.

Provide visual feedback when actions are completed (e.g., a button changes color when tapped, or a message confirms a successful submission). The easier it is for users to accomplish their goals, the more likely they are to return.

By grounding your design choices in these core principles—clarity, hierarchy, color, typography, and usability—you'll create an app experience that feels polished, purposeful, and enjoyable, even without advanced design training.

3.2 Wireframing and Prototyping: Use Free Tools Like Figma or Canva to Sketch Your App's Screens

Once you understand the design principles, the next step is to move from theory to structure—this is where wireframing and prototyping come into play. A **wireframe** is a simple, low-fidelity visual outline of your app's layout. It focuses on structure rather than style, showing where elements like buttons, menus, and content blocks will appear on each screen. A **prototype**, on the other hand, is a clickable model of your app that simulates how users will interact with it.

Wireframing is the blueprint of your app. It allows you to plan how each screen will function, what elements it will contain, and how users will navigate through your app. Think of it as sketching the skeleton of your user interface. At this stage, don't worry about colors, images, or branding. The goal is functionality and flow.

Several no-cost, beginner-friendly tools can help you wireframe your app digitally. **Figma**, for example, is a web-based design tool that offers a powerful set of features for wireframing and prototyping.

Its drag-and-drop interface, reusable components, and built-in collaboration features make it a favorite among professionals and beginners alike. **Canva**, while better known for graphic design, also offers simple tools for wireframing app screens. For those who prefer pen and paper, sketching your wireframes by hand is perfectly acceptable at this stage—what matters is that you're defining the layout.

To begin wireframing, start with your main screens—usually the home screen, a login or sign-up screen, the main feature interface, and a user profile or settings screen. Draw basic boxes to represent elements like headers, input fields, buttons, and content areas. Use arrows to indicate how users will navigate between screens. Keep asking yourself: "What does the user need to see? What action do I want them to take?"

After completing your wireframes, you can move into **prototyping**. This is where you make your wireframes interactive. Figma excels here, allowing you to link screens together using simple clicks. For instance, clicking a login button can take the user to the dashboard, while clicking "back" returns them to the previous screen. This clickable prototype mimics the real user experience, offering valuable insights into how your app feels in action.

Prototypes are a powerful tool for gathering feedback. Share your clickable prototype with friends, colleagues, or your intended users, and ask them to complete specific tasks—such as signing up, creating a profile, or using the core feature. Observe how they interact with the prototype. Where do they get stuck? What confuses them? These insights allow you to improve your design before investing time or money into development.

By wireframing and prototyping, you gain clarity, reduce risk, and make smarter design decisions. This phase transforms abstract ideas into tangible user experiences and gives you the confidence to move forward knowing your design is grounded in purpose and usability.

3.3 Choosing Your Design Aesthetic: Match Your Design with Your App's Tone and Audience

With your layout defined and your prototype in place, it's time to add style. This is where your app's

design aesthetic comes to life—the visual language that communicates your brand's identity and resonates with your users.

Your design aesthetic encompasses your color scheme, typography, imagery, and overall visual tone. Choosing the right aesthetic is not about copying trends or picking your favorite colors—it's about understanding your app's personality and the emotions you want to evoke in your users. This process begins with knowing your audience.

Ask yourself: Who are your users? Are they young professionals seeking productivity tools? Parents looking for family-friendly apps? Teenagers seeking entertainment? Each audience has distinct preferences and expectations. A fitness app aimed at millennials might use bold colors, dynamic fonts, and energetic imagery. A budgeting app for older adults might lean on calming hues, classic fonts, and a clean, straightforward layout.

Also, consider the **tone** of your app. Is it playful and fun? Serious and professional? Relaxing and meditative? Your aesthetic should reflect this tone. A playful app might use vibrant colors, rounded fonts, and whimsical icons. A professional app might use a minimal palette, sharp lines, and clean typography. Consistency across your design elements builds trust and creates a memorable user experience.

If you're unsure where to start, look for inspiration. Browse the App Store or Google Play and study apps in your niche. Notice the common themes in layout, color, and branding. Tools like **Dribbble** and **Behance** also offer thousands of examples of mobile app designs, which can help you refine your own vision.

When choosing your color palette, stick to a primary color, a secondary color, and one or two neutrals. Use your primary color for buttons and highlights, the secondary color for accents, and neutrals for backgrounds and text. Tools like **Coolors** or **Adobe**

Color can help you generate cohesive color schemes that look professional and polished.

Typography should reflect your app's tone and support readability. Choose no more than two font families—one for headings and one for body text. Make sure they scale well on different screen sizes, and always test for legibility.

Icons and images also play a role in your visual aesthetic. Use icons consistently throughout your app, and select a style—line, filled, flat, or skeuomorphic—and stick with it. For images, consider whether you'll use photographs, illustrations, or custom graphics. Ensure all visuals are high-quality and properly optimized for mobile screens.

Lastly, create a simple **style guide** for your app—a document that outlines your color palette, font choices, icon style, and image guidelines. This ensures consistency across screens and simplifies future updates or collaborations.

CHAPTER FOUR
Choosing the Right No-Code Platform

In the evolving world of digital creation, few movements have been as revolutionary as the rise of no-code platforms. These tools have made it possible for virtually anyone—with or without a background in computer science—to turn an idea into a functioning mobile or web application. If design brings your app to life visually, then no-code platforms breathe functionality into it.

They allow you to define workflows, build interfaces, and launch your product without ever writing a single line of code. Yet, with so many platforms available today—each with its own strengths and limitations—the challenge lies in selecting the one best suited to your unique project.

4.1 Understanding No-Code Options: Overview of Platforms Like Adalo, Glide, Thunkable, and Bubble

To begin, let's explore the no-code landscape by looking at four of the most popular and user-friendly platforms currently available: **Adalo, Glide, Thunkable,** and **Bubble**. Each of these tools has empowered thousands of entrepreneurs, small businesses, educators, and creatives to build mobile or web apps without hiring a development team.

Adalo is a no-code platform designed primarily for building native mobile apps. Its greatest strength lies in its intuitive drag-and-drop interface and strong visual editor. With Adalo, users can create fully functional apps complete with navigation, databases, and complex logic workflows.

It's ideal for those seeking a balance between ease of use and control over the app experience. You can publish directly to the App Store or Google Play, and the platform supports payment gateways, user authentication, and custom actions.

Glide is another popular choice, especially for creators who want to transform existing spreadsheets into sleek, data-driven apps. Glide works by connecting to Google Sheets, Airtable, or Excel and using your data as the backbone for the app.

It's particularly strong for internal tools, business dashboards, directories, and content-heavy apps. Its interface is polished, mobile-responsive, and extremely quick to build with. Glide is great for simplicity and speed, though it's more suited to lighter use cases than full-scale native apps.

Thunkable offers another layer of flexibility, especially for those who want to take a slightly more technical approach without fully diving into code. With a visual block-based programming system inspired by MIT's Scratch, Thunkable allows for more nuanced app behaviors and interactions.

It's an excellent choice for building cross-platform apps that require complex logic or custom components. You can test your app on your phone in real-time and publish to both major app stores with ease.

Bubble, while traditionally geared more toward web apps than mobile, is by far the most powerful no-code platform in terms of backend logic, data manipulation, and user experience design. Bubble allows complete customization, intricate workflows, and real-time databases.

While its learning curve is a bit steeper than the others, it opens up possibilities previously reserved for traditional coding. It's the go-to platform for those looking to build scalable startups, marketplaces, or SaaS platforms without developers.

Together, these platforms cover a broad range of use cases—from simple internal apps to complex consumer-facing products. Your task, then, is not just to learn about them, but to determine which one is best for your project's needs, ambitions, and growth potential.

4.2 Platform Matchmaking: How to Choose the Right Tool for Your App's Complexity

Choosing a no-code platform isn't about picking the one with the most features. It's about selecting the tool that matches the complexity and purpose of your app while aligning with your technical comfort level and long-term goals.

Start by revisiting your app's **core purpose**. Is it a basic utility, a business tool, a marketplace, or a community-driven platform? If you're building something like a simple event planner or employee directory, Glide might be a perfect fit. But if your app requires deeper interactivity, like user-specific dashboards or gamification, Adalo or Thunkable might be more appropriate.

For highly dynamic and customizable platforms— like Airbnb-style marketplaces—Bubble may be the only one with enough firepower.

Complexity is the next major factor. Ask yourself a few guiding questions:

- Does my app need to store user data?
- Will it require account creation and login functionality?
- Do I need payments, subscriptions, or notifications?
- Will users interact with each other (messaging, profiles, reviews)?
- Will the app grow significantly in scope over time?

The more "yes" answers you give, the more powerful a platform you'll need. Adalo and Thunkable, for example, support user logins and databases but handle logic differently. Thunkable gives more control via visual programming, while Adalo's logic system is better for beginners. Glide is perfect for displaying and editing structured data but struggles with more advanced logic. Bubble, meanwhile, is built to handle virtually all of these requirements, albeit with a more time-intensive learning process.

Your **timeline and learning style** also matter. If you need to launch quickly or prefer a visual, simplified approach, Glide and Adalo are user-friendly and offer faster build cycles. If you enjoy experimenting, learning systems, and gaining more creative control, then Bubble's steep but rewarding curve may suit you better. Thunkable strikes a balance between both worlds.

Budget is another factor, especially if you're bootstrapping your app idea. All four platforms offer free plans with basic functionality, but most meaningful features—like custom domains, app store deployment, or database size—are locked behind paid plans. Glide's pricing is generous for internal or prototype apps, while Bubble's becomes cost-effective only when you scale. Adalo and Thunkable also offer scalable pricing, but publishing to app stores often requires a paid tier.

Lastly, consider **community and support**. Check out forums, documentation, YouTube tutorials, and templates. Platforms with active communities and robust educational content can significantly shorten your learning curve.

In sum, platform matchmaking is about thoughtful alignment—not just of features, but of your app's intended use, your growth ambitions, and your comfort level. The best no-code platform for you is the one that empowers you to build confidently, iterate quickly, and launch without overwhelming complexity.

4.3 Setting Up Your Workspace: Register, Organize Your Project, and Prepare to Build

Once you've selected your platform, the next step is to set up your development workspace—a clean, organized digital environment where your app will begin to take form. The process is simple but crucial. A thoughtful setup saves you time, prevents confusion, and helps you stay focused as your project evolves.

Start by **registering** for your chosen platform. Most no-code tools only require an email and password to create an account. Once registered, you'll be taken to your dashboard—the central hub where you can manage projects, settings, templates, and more.

Create a **new project**, usually by clicking a button labeled "Create New App" or something similar. At this point, you may be asked to choose between different templates or start from scratch. While templates can be helpful, especially for beginners, starting with a blank slate often provides a better understanding of your app's structure. Give your project a meaningful name—something that clearly identifies the app's function or working title.

Next, **organize your project's structure**. Most platforms allow you to create pages or screens, define navigation paths, and set up databases or components. Begin by creating the core screens you outlined during the wireframing stage: the home screen, login/signup screen, feature screens, and settings/profile screen.

Create folders or label groups to keep assets—like images, icons, or content—neatly organized. In Bubble, for example, you'll define your database structure upfront, creating fields and data types that match your app's needs. In Glide, you'll format your spreadsheet with the correct headers. In Thunkable and Adalo, you can create "collections" or "data tables" to manage your app's content.

This is also the time to **define your user roles and logic**. Will users see different content based on their status? Do they need to register before accessing key features? Set up user workflows accordingly. Most platforms provide visual workflows or logic editors to control what happens when users click buttons, input data, or navigate between screens.

Once the basic structure is in place, begin **importing assets**—logos, images, icons, and colors defined in your design aesthetic. Apply your style guide consistently across screens to establish a strong visual identity. Set up navigation menus, onboarding flows, and the main layout for each screen.

Finally, take time to **test your setup**. Use the preview or live testing features to simulate how the app looks and behaves on a mobile device. Fix any layout issues, adjust buttons, and ensure transitions feel smooth.

Even at this early stage, testing is critical—it helps you catch problems early and keeps you grounded in the user experience.

CHAPTER FIVE
Building Your App (Part 1) – Pages, Navigation & Layout

In the world of app development, functionality and design must go hand in hand to create a smooth, engaging user experience. While earlier chapters focused on refining your app idea, choosing the right platform, and establishing a visual identity, this chapter marks the transition from planning to doing. You are now ready to begin building. And in the world of no-code development, this is where the fun truly begins.

This first phase of actual app construction revolves around three foundational elements: creating screens and pages, adding navigation and menus, and structuring the layout in a way that feels clean, simple, and intuitive to your users.

In many ways, this phase is the skeleton of your app—these are the bones upon which all features, content, and design will be layered. Getting this right sets the stage for a seamless experience and ensures that your future updates, features, and improvements will rest on a strong framework.

Let's begin the build with the creation of screens, the addition of navigation, and the layout principles that bring everything together in a polished, professional manner.

5.1 Creating Screens and Pages: Learn to Add and Arrange Screens Using Drag-and-Drop Builders

Every app begins as a collection of individual screens—each one serving a specific purpose. In a no-code platform, these screens are created using intuitive drag-and-drop tools, allowing you to visually design and connect the different parts of your app without technical complexity.

Think of your screens as digital canvases. On each canvas, you'll place different elements—text, images, buttons, forms, and more—to accomplish a specific goal. Some screens will be static, like an

About page or a Welcome screen, while others will be interactive, such as a user dashboard or a product listing.

Most no-code platforms offer a "New Screen" or "Add Page" function, usually accessible from the sidebar or main project dashboard. Begin by identifying the core screens your app will need based on your earlier planning and wireframes. At minimum, this often includes a Home screen, Login or Signup page, a few Feature-specific screens (like Task Lists or Profile), and Settings or Help sections.

Once the screens are created, arrange them in a logical order. Most platforms allow you to drag and rearrange pages in your workspace or display them in a flowchart-like structure. This visual map of your app gives you an overview of how users will progress from one screen to another.

It's important to name your screens clearly—avoid generic labels like "Page 1" or "New Page." Use descriptive names such as "Main Menu," "User

Profile," or "Order Confirmation." This not only helps you stay organized but also makes your app easier to manage as it grows.

Using the drag-and-drop builder, begin to add content blocks onto your screens. A typical screen may include a header at the top, a content area in the middle, and a footer at the bottom.

Components like buttons, cards, text fields, and images can be placed with simple clicks and dragged into place. Most no-code tools offer alignment guides and spacing controls to keep everything tidy.

Don't worry about perfection at this stage. Focus on building out the full set of pages your app will need. The details—fonts, colors, animations—can be refined later. What matters most now is creating a complete structure that can support your app's features and user journey.

5.2 Adding Navigation and Menus: Set Up Menus, Back Buttons, and Intuitive Flow

Once your screens are created, the next task is to make them connect. Navigation is what transforms a collection of pages into a cohesive, flowing app experience. It's also a key contributor to how users perceive the professionalism and usability of your app.

Start by understanding the two primary types of navigation: **top-level navigation** and **contextual navigation**. Top-level navigation refers to consistent menu options that help users switch between major sections of your app. This could be a bottom tab bar (like in Instagram), a top bar (like in Gmail), or a side drawer menu (common in Android apps).

Contextual navigation, on the other hand, includes in-screen links or buttons that move the user forward or backward in the app's flow.

Most no-code platforms have pre-built navigation components—tab bars, menu lists, hamburger icons, and navigation buttons. These components can be dragged onto your screens and customized. For example, if you're building an app in Adalo or Thunkable, you can add a bottom navigation bar with icons for Home, Explore, Messages, and Profile, each linking to a corresponding screen.

Linking between pages is usually done through "actions" or "events." When a user taps a button or swipes left, an action is triggered that sends them to another screen. This flow should be logical and easy to follow.

For example, from the Home screen, the user might tap "Create New Task," which takes them to a form page. After submitting the form, they're returned to a confirmation screen or back to the list.

Back buttons are essential, especially in apps with multi-step processes. Many no-code tools automatically add back navigation to the top-left of a screen, but it's always wise to test this. Users expect to be able to return to a previous step easily, and any friction here can lead to frustration and app abandonment.

Menus should also be clean and minimal. Avoid overloading your navigation bar with too many options. A good rule of thumb is to limit top-level tabs to four or five items. Submenus and expandable lists can be used for secondary options like Settings, FAQ, or Logout.

Consider accessibility and ease of use when designing your menus. Use clear labels and icons that users can understand without explanation. Keep interactions consistent across screens—if tapping a plus icon adds a new item on one screen, it should do the same on others.

Navigation is more than just functionality—it shapes how your users experience your app. A clear, intuitive navigation system keeps users confident and engaged, encouraging them to explore and return again.

5.3 Structuring Your App for Simplicity: Keep Your Layout Clean and User-Friendly

With screens and navigation in place, the final step in this foundational phase is to structure each part of your app for maximum simplicity. A clean, user-friendly layout is one of the most powerful indicators of a well-built app. It shows that you care about the user experience and understand the importance of design in function.

Simplicity begins with focus. Each screen should have one primary purpose. Avoid cluttering the interface with too many buttons, options, or blocks of text. If a user opens a screen to check their to-do list, don't distract them with unrelated news, ads, or secondary features. Focus helps the user achieve their goal faster and with less mental effort.

Use spacing generously. White space isn't empty space—it's breathing room. It helps users process content more easily and creates a more modern, aesthetically pleasing design. Use padding and margins to separate components clearly. Group related items together (like name and email fields in a form) and separate unrelated elements.

Typography plays a big role in clarity. Use font sizes and weights to create visual hierarchy—larger, bolder text for titles, medium-sized text for instructions, and smaller text for labels or descriptions. Avoid using too many fonts or colors, which can make the app look chaotic.

Stick to a limited color palette that matches your brand or mood. Choose one primary color (for buttons and highlights), a secondary color (for accents), and neutral tones for backgrounds and text. Too many colors can be distracting and dilute your brand identity.

Icons and images should support, not replace, your content. Use icons where appropriate—like a trash icon for delete or a pencil icon for edit—but always pair them with text unless the meaning is obvious. For example, a heart icon might imply "like" to some users but confuse others. Adding labels ensures clarity.

Responsiveness is another key aspect of a good layout. Your app should look and function well on different screen sizes and orientations. Most no-code platforms let you preview how your app will appear on various devices. Test your layout regularly, especially after adding new elements.

Remember, users don't think in terms of screens and components—they experience your app as a whole. The best layout is one that feels effortless to use. Every tap, swipe, and scroll should feel natural and frictionless.

CHAPTER SIX
Building Your App (Part 2) – Features and Functionality

With your app's structure in place—pages built, navigation set, and layout thoughtfully arranged—it's now time to infuse your creation with the features that make it useful, interactive, and engaging. This stage is where your app becomes more than just a digital shell. It evolves into a tool that users can interact with, rely on, and return to.

No-code platforms have revolutionized the way features are added to mobile apps. What once required complex programming can now be achieved with drag-and-drop logic and simple configuration panels. You can now incorporate forms, create dynamic content displays, and integrate media or external tools—all without writing a single line of code.

This chapter explores three critical areas: capturing user input through forms and actions, displaying dynamic content such as lists or cards, and enriching your app with advanced capabilities like media handling, map services, and third-party integrations. These functionalities are what give your app depth and make it truly responsive to user needs.

6.1 Input Forms and User Interactions: Learn How Users Can Enter Data or Perform Actions

User interaction is the cornerstone of any mobile app. Whether it's signing up, submitting a review, creating a task, or sending a message, your users need to input data to engage with your app's features. Fortunately, most no-code platforms offer intuitive tools for building robust and responsive forms.

To start, consider what kind of data your app needs to collect. A fitness tracking app may ask for user weight and exercise logs; a social app might require profile photos and bio details; an ordering app could need delivery addresses and payment preferences. Each of these tasks involves some form of user input, and that begins with designing forms.

In a no-code builder like Adalo, Glide, or Thunkable, you can insert prebuilt form components onto any screen. These typically include fields like text inputs, email fields, password inputs, dropdown menus, checkboxes, and date pickers. You can drag these fields onto the screen and arrange them in the order you want the user to complete them.

Beyond merely collecting input, effective forms must be user-friendly and visually consistent. Keep the number of fields to a minimum—only ask for what you absolutely need. Use clear labels, placeholder text, and helpful error messages. For example, if a user tries to submit a form without filling in a required field, your app should gently alert them and explain what's missing.

Actions and conditions bring interactivity to the next level. In many platforms, you can configure what happens when a form is submitted. This might include saving the data to a backend database, sending an email notification, or redirecting the user to a confirmation screen. You can also set up conditional visibility—only showing certain fields if a previous selection warrants it. For instance, if a user selects "Other" as a reason for feedback, a follow-up text box can appear asking for more detail.

Another important form of interaction is using buttons or gestures to trigger actions. Buttons can be linked to a wide variety of tasks: opening new screens, updating data, toggling visibility of an element, or initiating an integration.

These actions are usually set up through visual workflows or logic builders, which allow you to design the app's behavior step by step.

In sum, input forms and user interaction features are what turn your app from a display of content into a functional system. It's how users make the app their own, personalize their experience, and participate in the digital ecosystem you've created.

6.2 Displaying Dynamic Content: Use Lists, Cards, and Filters to Show Changing Data

While forms let users provide input, dynamic content allows you to reflect that input back to them in meaningful ways. Dynamic content refers to any part of your app that changes based on the data—such as a list of tasks, profiles, events, or items added by users.

In most no-code tools, this is achieved by linking screens and components to a database or collection. For instance, if you're building a recipe app, you might have a database called "Recipes" containing fields like name, ingredients, and image. You can then create a screen that displays this content as a scrollable list or grid of recipe cards.

Components like lists, cards, and tables can be dragged onto a screen and configured to automatically pull from your app's data. These components will update in real-time as new data is added or changed. You don't need to manually update anything; the system does it for you.

Let's take the example of a task management app. A "Tasks" database stores each user's tasks, including titles, deadlines, and completion status. A list component on the home screen could display all tasks that are not yet marked as complete. Each item in the list can be customized to show icons, colors, or buttons (e.g., "Mark as Done") that update the record when tapped.

Filtering and sorting are powerful features that enhance usability. Filters allow users to view only the content relevant to them. For example, users could filter a product list by price range, category, or availability. In Glide, you can apply filters directly within the design interface—only show items where the status is "Available," or only show posts created by the logged-in user.

Sorting ensures content is shown in a logical order— most recent, alphabetical, by popularity, etc.

Pagination or infinite scroll can also be used to improve performance and avoid overwhelming the user with too much data at once.

Dynamic content also improves personalization. By using conditions based on user profiles or preferences, you can tailor what each user sees. For example, a language-learning app might show lessons based on the user's skill level, or a fitness app might suggest workouts based on previously entered goals.

Ultimately, dynamic content is what makes your app feel alive. It reflects the evolving needs, preferences, and inputs of your users in real-time, creating a more relevant and engaging experience.

6.3 Working with Media, Maps, and Integrations: Add Rich Features Like Photos, Videos, or Maps

Today's users expect apps to go beyond text and buttons. Media and integrations provide a way to add richness, versatility, and real-world utility to your app. From photos and videos to maps and third-party services, these elements can elevate the user experience significantly.

Let's begin with **media**. Whether you want users to upload profile pictures, view tutorial videos, or browse photo galleries, media features are essential. No-code platforms typically allow you to add image and video components directly to your screens. You can pull images from your database or let users upload their own.

When allowing uploads, be mindful of privacy and file size limitations. Platforms like Adalo or Glide allow for secure file storage, but it's important to set rules—for example, limiting upload formats or file sizes. Thumbnails and image previews can enhance the visual layout and make the app feel more interactive.

Video is a powerful medium, especially for instructional or marketing apps. Most platforms let you embed videos using YouTube or Vimeo links.

Alternatively, some tools allow native video hosting if you're using their premium tiers. Position your videos strategically—on welcome screens, help sections, or as part of user onboarding flows.

Maps are another feature that adds immense value to location-based apps. Whether you're building a delivery app, a travel planner, or a service locator, interactive maps can greatly enhance utility. Many no-code platforms offer map components that integrate with Google Maps or Mapbox.

You can drop pins, show routes, or even filter map results based on user location. For example, a local business directory app can display nearby stores on a map, using data from your "Business" database that includes latitude and longitude fields. Users can click on map markers to open detail pages, call the business, or get directions.

Finally, **integrations** allow your app to connect with external tools and services. This is where no-code truly shines. Through platforms like Zapier, Make (formerly Integromat), or built-in connectors, you can automate workflows between your app and services like Gmail, Google Sheets, Airtable, Slack, and more.

Suppose you're building a booking app. You can set up an integration where, every time a user makes a booking, the data is sent to a Google Sheet, an email confirmation is triggered, and a Slack message alerts the admin. These tasks can be automated with minimal setup.

Integrations also expand your app's capabilities. Want to send push notifications? Use OneSignal. Want to collect payments? Integrate Stripe or PayPal. Want user authentication through social login? Many platforms now support Google or Facebook login with just a few configuration steps.

Rich features make your app feel modern and professional. They help you stand out in a crowded marketplace and give your users tools that make their lives easier. As with all things in design, use them purposefully. Just because a feature is available doesn't mean it should be used. Focus on what serves your user best.

CHAPTER SEVEN
Managing Data – Backends, Databases, and Storage

As your mobile app begins to take shape, with screens built and user interactions embedded, it's time to address one of the most important and often misunderstood aspects of app development: data management. Behind every functional app lies a structured foundation of data—how it's stored, how it's retrieved, how it's updated, and how it connects to the visual components of the user interface.

Whether you're building a social network, a task manager, or an e-commerce tool, managing your app's data intelligently ensures a smooth user experience and long-term scalability.

Unlike traditional programming, which complex server setups and SQL queries, no-code platforms simplify data management through intuitive tools and built-in backends. These platforms allow you to focus more on what your app does than how it functions technically.

7.1 Choosing a Simple Backend: Understand Airtable, Google Sheets, or Built-in Databases

The backend is essentially the brain of your application. It's where all your app's data is stored and processed, allowing you to save user input, manage dynamic content, and retrieve information when needed.

In traditional development, setting up a backend often involves configuring servers and databases like MySQL or MongoDB. But in the no-code world, you have access to simplified solutions like Airtable, Google Sheets, or native app builder databases— each with unique strengths.

Airtable has become a favorite among no-code developers due to its familiar spreadsheet interface combined with the power of a relational database. You can organize data into multiple tables, link records between them, and even attach files or images to rows. Airtable also supports powerful filtering, sorting, and automation rules. It's a great choice when your app needs moderate complexity, like linking user profiles to specific tasks or creating categorized lists of content. Airtable's API makes it easy to connect with platforms like Glide, Adalo, or Bubble.

Google Sheets is another popular option, especially for beginners. It feels just like using Excel—rows, columns, and cells—so the learning curve is minimal. Many no-code platforms offer built-in connectors for Google Sheets, making it ideal for simpler apps or prototypes.

For instance, if you're building a basic inventory management tool, you can store all items in a Google Sheet and sync them with your app in real time. However, because it isn't designed for relational data or complex logic, it may not be the best choice for more advanced use cases.

Built-in databases, offered by platforms like Adalo and Glide, are the most seamless way to manage app data without leaving the app builder environment. These databases are tightly integrated into the platform's UI, allowing you to create tables, define relationships, and manage entries directly within the editor.

This approach minimizes technical barriers and is perfect for first-time builders who want to keep everything in one place. The downside is that you may have limited flexibility or scalability compared to external solutions like Airtable.

Ultimately, the best backend for your app depends on its complexity and purpose. For a robust multi-user application with linked data, Airtable might be the best fit.

For fast prototypes and small projects, Google Sheets is a reliable choice. And for streamlined simplicity, native platform databases offer everything you need to get started.

7.2 Connecting Your Data to the UI: Link Visual Elements to Live Content

Once you've chosen your backend and set up your data tables, the next step is to connect your data to your app's user interface (UI). This is where the magic happens—transforming raw data into dynamic visuals that update in real time as users interact with your app. This process is crucial because your app's usability and responsiveness depend on how effectively it reflects the underlying data.

In a no-code environment, this connection is typically established through **data bindings**. Data bindings are the links between a visual component—like a text box, image, list, or button—and a specific field in your database.

Let's say you're building a recipe app and you have a "Recipes" database table. You might create a card component for each recipe and bind the title, image, and description fields from the table to elements in the card. When your database updates (e.g., a new recipe is added), the UI updates automatically.

Lists and repeatable components are commonly used to display multiple records from a database. For instance, if you have a list of users, a repeatable row might display each user's name and profile picture. The app fetches each entry from your database and populates the visual elements accordingly. You can further enhance the UI by adding sorting rules (e.g., display newest items first) or filters (e.g., show only items created by the current user).

Buttons and interactive elements can also be linked to data actions. For example, tapping a "Delete" button can trigger the removal of a database entry, or selecting a dropdown menu can update a user's profile preference. These actions are often set up using **workflow builders**, which allow you to define what happens when a user performs an action.

Conditional visibility is another powerful feature. You can choose to show or hide certain UI elements based on the state of your data. For example, if a user has not filled out their profile, you can display a "Complete Profile" prompt. Once their data is updated, that prompt disappears automatically.

This live connection between data and UI ensures that your app remains dynamic and personalized. Instead of static content, users are presented with real-time updates tailored to their actions, needs, and preferences—making your app feel smarter, faster, and more intuitive.

7.3 Creating, Reading, Updating, Deleting (CRUD): Learn Basic Data Operations in No-Code

The cornerstone of every database-driven app lies in mastering CRUD operations—Create, Read, Update, and Delete. These operations define how data moves through your app and how users interact with the information stored behind the scenes. In a no-code context, these operations are not written in code but are performed through visual logic builders, drag-and-drop functions, and pre-set actions.

Create operations occur when a user inputs new information into your app. For instance, when someone registers for your app, submits a form, or adds a new task, they're creating a new entry in your database.

On platforms like Adalo or Glide, you can configure a "Submit" button to take all form inputs and save them as a new record in a specific data table. Most platforms allow you to automatically add timestamps, user identifiers, or unique IDs for each new entry.

Read operations are how your app displays existing data to users. Any time you display content from your backend—like a user's profile, a news feed, or a shopping cart—you are reading from the database.

This is typically done using list or card components, as discussed earlier, which pull in and display real-time data. You can control what data is shown through filters, user-specific rules, and dynamic conditions.

Update operations allow users to modify existing data. For example, editing a profile, marking a task as complete, or changing a setting. This often involves two steps: first, retrieving the existing data and displaying it in editable fields; and second, saving the new values back to the database when the user submits changes.

Platforms like Bubble and Thunkable offer workflows for defining exactly which fields to update and when.

A common example is allowing users to edit their own posts. You would pull in their original data into a form, let them make changes, and then save the updates. You can also set visibility conditions so users can only edit their own content, not others'.

Delete operations remove data from the backend. While powerful, they should be used cautiously. Most no-code platforms allow you to attach delete actions to buttons, swipe gestures, or menus. It's best practice to include a confirmation prompt before actually deleting data, to prevent accidental removal.

Some platforms support **soft deletes**, where data is not permanently erased but flagged as "deleted." This allows for recovery or auditing. You can implement this by having a "deleted" field in your table and filtering it out from views, rather than removing the record entirely.

Mastering CRUD operations enables your app to be fully functional, empowering users to not only consume content but to contribute, edit, and manage it. This interaction turns your app into a living system—constantly evolving based on user activity and data flow.

CHAPTER EIGHT

Testing and Feedback – Making It Smooth and Bug-Free

After months of brainstorming, designing, and building, it's finally time to test your app. But testing isn't just about fixing bugs—it's a crucial process to ensure that your app delivers a seamless and enjoyable user experience.

In the previous chapters, you've focused on laying the foundation and adding functionality to your app. Now, it's time to make sure everything works as expected and that your users can navigate through your app effortlessly, without encountering glitches, confusion, or frustration.

This chapter will guide you through the process of testing your app, gathering meaningful feedback, and iterating based on insights. You'll learn how to simulate real-world use cases, collect feedback from test users, and use that feedback to make informed improvements. Through thoughtful testing and careful iteration, you will refine your app into a polished, bug-free experience ready for launch.

8.1 Testing Like a User: Simulate Real Use Cases to Spot Flaws or Frustrations

When testing your app, it's easy to fall into the trap of thinking everything works simply because you built it. However, as the creator, you have a different perspective than the average user. You understand the flow, the features, and the logic behind everything. But your users don't have this insight—they interact with your app based on their own expectations and experience.

To truly understand your app's usability, you must test it like a user. This means simulating real-world use cases to ensure the app performs as expected across a variety of scenarios. A crucial part of this process is **thinking through the user journey**.

Start from the very beginning—imagine a first-time user launching the app for the first time, signing up, and completing an action. How easy or difficult is it for them to figure out how to navigate? Do they experience any friction at any point?

Real-life testing scenarios could include tasks such as:

- Navigating through the app's main features without prior knowledge of the interface.
- Completing tasks or using features that aren't immediately obvious to new users, like filtering data, using menus, or accessing secondary screens.
- Testing edge cases, like logging in with incorrect information or attempting to perform actions without a stable internet connection.

The key here is to simulate a variety of realistic situations. You might feel that your app works fine in most cases, but by playing the role of a typical user, you might uncover hidden problems—such as navigation confusion, unresponsive buttons, or poor performance during high usage. Simulating real-world usage and interactions will help you spot these flaws early on.

Another critical element in testing is **device diversity**. People use apps across various devices, including smartphones, tablets, and even different screen sizes. Testing your app on multiple devices or emulators ensures that it looks and functions well across the board.

Some elements may not appear correctly on smaller screens, or your app's layout may break when displayed on larger screens. By testing on various device sizes and operating systems (Android and iOS), you'll ensure that your app delivers a consistent experience for all users.

While performing these tests, keep track of your findings. Take notes on the issues you encounter, and be as specific as possible in identifying problems. If possible, use tools like **screen recording** or **session replay software** to capture your experience. This will allow you to analyze the flow and pinpoint any friction points more accurately.

8.2 Getting External Feedback: Share a Prototype or Preview with Friends and Test Users

Once you've gone through your own internal testing, it's time to share your app with others. At this stage, external feedback is invaluable. It's easy to be blinded by your own work and miss potential usability issues. Getting fresh perspectives from friends, family, and strangers—who will interact with your app without any bias or prior knowledge—can provide invaluable insights.

Sharing a prototype or preview with potential users allows them to experience the app as an outsider. Whether you've created a simple wireframe or a fully functional prototype, inviting external users to test it will provide you with actionable feedback. You can choose between a few methods of sharing your app:

1. **Private Testing Groups**: You can invite a small, curated group of users—whether friends, family, or colleagues—to test your app. These testers should represent a variety of experience levels and technical backgrounds to ensure that their feedback encompasses a broad range of perspectives.

2. **Beta Testing**: Many no-code platforms, such as Adalo, Bubble, or Glide, offer beta testing features that allow you to share your app with a larger group of users. Beta testers will typically provide feedback on specific areas of the app, and you may ask them to focus on certain tasks or aspects that you suspect could be problematic.

3. **Public Prototyping Tools**: Tools like Figma, InVision, or Marvel allow you to share interactive prototypes with others, which can help you gather feedback without having to build the full app. Prototypes allow users to interact with the design and provide suggestions before the app is fully developed.

When seeking feedback, it's important to approach it systematically. Instead of just asking, "What do you think of the app?" focus on specific areas that might need refinement. Consider asking questions like:

- Was it easy to navigate through the app? Were there any moments where you felt lost?
- Did any feature seem confusing or unnecessary?
- Were there any technical issues (e.g., slow loading, crashes, unresponsive elements)?
- How would you improve the overall user experience?

Make sure to offer an easy way for users to provide feedback, whether through surveys, comment sections, or in-person interviews. You can also leverage **user experience (UX) surveys** to collect more structured feedback about design elements, layout, and features.

External feedback also helps you identify bugs or issues that you might have missed during your internal testing. A fresh set of eyes is often the best way to uncover these problems.

Whether it's a glitch in a button that doesn't work or an awkward user flow, external feedback provides the necessary clues for improvements.

8.3 Iterating Based on Insights: Adjust Your App with Clarity Based on Feedback

Once you've gathered feedback from both internal testing and external users, it's time to start iterating. Iteration is the process of refining your app based on the feedback you've received. It's not just about fixing bugs—it's about enhancing the user experience, improving usability, and optimizing features.

Clarity and focus are key during this phase. When reviewing the feedback, categorize the issues based on severity and impact. Some problems will need immediate attention—such as critical bugs or broken features—while others might be less urgent but important for the overall user experience. Don't try to fix everything at once. Instead, prioritize adjustments that will have the most significant impact on user satisfaction and usability.

Consider the following approach for effective iteration:

- **Address usability issues first**: Focus on areas where users are experiencing frustration or confusion. If users are struggling to find a particular feature or are getting lost in the app's flow, simplify the design or add helpful cues like tooltips, labels, or onboarding screens.
- **Fix critical bugs and glitches**: Address any bugs that cause the app to crash or hinder essential functionality. Technical stability is essential for user retention, and a bug-free experience is a must for building credibility and trust with your users.
- **Refine features and design**: Once the basics are covered, move on to refining the design and functionality. Adjust features that users

didn't fully understand or didn't find useful. Sometimes, users will point out that a particular feature is unnecessary or redundant—consider removing or consolidating these features to keep the app streamlined and easy to use.

- **Conduct another round of testing**: Once you've implemented changes, test your app again, either with the same group of users or with new testers. This second round of testing allows you to evaluate the changes you've made and ensure that new problems haven't emerged.

This iterative process should be repeated as needed until your app is polished and bug-free. Keep in mind that every feedback loop makes your app better. And the more user-centered your testing and iteration process, the more likely you are to create an app that meets the needs of your audience.

CHAPTER NINE
Launching Your App – Going Live

The moment you've been waiting for has arrived. After months of planning, designing, and building, your app is finally ready for the world to see. But before you can sit back and relax, there's one crucial step left: launching your app.

This chapter will guide you through the process of launching your app-to-app stores or the web, providing you with essential steps to ensure a smooth and successful launch.

9.1 Preparing for the App Store: Add Metadata, Icons, Screenshots, and Compliance

Before your app is officially available for download, there's an array of behind-the-scenes tasks to complete. These steps ensure that your app meets the requirements of the app stores and is properly presented to your audience.

Preparing for the app store involves a combination of technical setups, design considerations, and legal compliance checks.

Metadata is the first thing users will see when they come across your app in the app store. This includes your app's name, description, keywords, and category. Crafting a compelling app description is crucial, as it serves as the primary marketing tool for your app.

Here, you'll want to clearly explain what your app does, why it's valuable, and how it solves the problems your target users face. Keep the tone concise and persuasive, and remember to incorporate relevant keywords to boost discoverability in search results.

Along with your app's description, **app icons** and **screenshots** play a significant role in attracting users. App icons should be visually striking and instantly recognizable, while screenshots should showcase your app's key features and functionality.

Think of these visual elements as the window through which users will view your app. A well-designed icon and an eye-catching set of screenshots can dramatically increase your app's download rate.

Compliance is another critical aspect of preparing for the app store. Different app stores have various guidelines and rules that your app must adhere to, especially when it comes to user data protection, privacy policies, and age ratings. You must ensure that your app complies with these rules, or it may face rejection during the submission process.

For example, Apple's App Store and Google Play both require privacy policies if your app collects any personal user data. Make sure to create a clear and transparent privacy policy and include it in your app's metadata.

Also, remember that both Apple and Google have specific guidelines regarding app functionality, content, and design. For instance, Apple emphasizes a polished, native-like experience, while Google

Play focuses on performance and user experience. Ensure that your app meets the respective guidelines for the platform you're publishing on to avoid delays or rejection.

Finally, **app localization** is an essential consideration if you plan to expand your app's reach. By localizing your app, you can provide your app in multiple languages, making it accessible to a broader, global audience.

Depending on the region, users may expect apps in their native language, and localization will allow your app to be more appealing to different cultural and linguistic groups.

9.2 Publishing to Google Play or the Web: Steps to Go Live with No-Code Platforms

Once your app is fully prepared and ready for release, it's time to publish. With no-code platforms like Adalo, Glide, Thunkable, and Bubble, the process of going live is much simpler compared to traditional app development.

These platforms handle much of the backend work, allowing you to focus on the creative and functional aspects of your app.

Publishing to Google Play involves a series of straightforward steps that include setting up your developer account, preparing your APK (Android Package) file, and submitting your app to the Google Play Store.

If you're using a no-code platform, much of this process is automated, and you can generate the APK file with just a few clicks. However, there are still important steps to follow.

1. **Create a Developer Account**: Before submitting your app to Google Play, you need to create a Google Play Developer Account. This account comes with a one-time registration fee (currently $25), and it will give you access to the Google Play Console, where you can manage your app's listings, updates, and analytics.

2. **Generate the APK File**: Using your no-code platform, generate the APK file for your app. The APK file is what users will download and install on their Android devices. Ensure that the APK is properly configured and free of errors before submission.

3. **Submit Your App**: Once you've uploaded your APK to the Google Play Console, it's time to complete your app's listing. You'll need to provide all the metadata—such as the app's name, description, and screenshots—as well as add any additional details required by Google, like your privacy policy, rating, and categorization.

4. **App Review and Approval**: After submission, Google will review your app to ensure it complies with its guidelines. This review process typically takes a few days but can sometimes take longer depending on the complexity of your app. If your app passes the review, it will be published on the Google Play Store.

Publishing to the Web is often a simpler and quicker process, especially for apps designed for desktop or mobile browsers. Many no-code platforms offer easy options to deploy your app directly to the web without needing to navigate the app store submission process.

For example, platforms like Glide allow you to create a progressive web app (PWA) that can be accessed via any browser, while platforms like Adalo allow you to generate a web version of your app directly.

Here's how to publish a web app:

1. **Export Your App to the Web**: In your no-code platform's dashboard, select the option to publish your app to the web. You will typically be able to choose between creating a public URL or linking the app to your own custom domain.

2. **Custom Domain (Optional)**: If you want a more professional and branded experience, you can connect your app to a custom

domain. Many no-code platforms offer simple tools to link your app to a domain name, or you can use an external service like Google Domains or GoDaddy.

3. **Test Your App on the Web**: Before going live, thoroughly test your app on different browsers and devices to ensure that it functions correctly and displays as expected across all platforms. Browser testing tools like BrowserStack can help you simulate different environments and detect issues.

4. **Go Live**: Once everything is set, simply hit the "publish" button, and your app will be live on the web for anyone to access. You can promote your app via social media, email marketing, or any other method that suits your strategy.

9.3 What to Expect After Launch: Set Expectations for Downloads, Updates, and User Feedback

The excitement of going live is palpable, but the work doesn't stop once your app is published. Launching your app is just the beginning of the journey. While it's natural to expect a flood of downloads and users right away, the reality is that growth takes time and strategic effort.

After launch, you should expect a **gradual increase in downloads** as word of your app spreads. It's unlikely that you will see instant success, especially if you don't have a built-in user base or a significant marketing campaign in place.

You can expect a period of discovery as users find your app through the app stores, word of mouth, and marketing efforts. Don't be discouraged if your initial download numbers are modest. With persistence and continuous improvements, your app can build momentum over time.

User feedback is another crucial part of the post-launch phase. Once users start interacting with your app, they will inevitably have feedback—both positive and negative. Pay close attention to reviews and ratings on the app store, as they offer valuable insights into user experiences.

Negative reviews can feel disheartening, but they provide critical information on what needs fixing. Addressing user complaints and concerns is key to improving your app's reputation and retention.

One of the best ways to collect feedback is through **in-app surveys** or feedback forms. By asking users to share their thoughts directly within the app, you can collect feedback in real time.

Be sure to thank users for their input and let them know that you are listening. Responding to reviews and engaging with your users shows that you care about their experience and are committed to improving your app.

App updates will also play a significant role in maintaining user engagement. Even after launch, your app will require regular updates to fix bugs, introduce new features, and ensure compatibility with the latest operating systems and devices. A consistent update schedule keeps your app fresh and ensures that users are satisfied with its performance.

Finally, **marketing efforts** are essential to ensure long-term success. You should consider employing various strategies like search engine optimization (SEO), app store optimization (ASO), and social media marketing to reach your target audience.

Consider offering incentives like referral programs or limited-time promotions to encourage users to download and share your app.

CHAPTER TEN
Growing Beyond Launch – Marketing, Updates, and Monetization

The journey of creating and launching an app is undoubtedly thrilling. However, the true challenge begins once your app is live. While the launch is a significant milestone, it's only the first step in a long process of growth and success. To ensure that your app reaches its full potential, you need to focus on key areas: marketing, maintaining app quality, and finding ways to generate revenue.

10.1 Promoting Your App on a Budget: Use Social Media, Free PR, and App Directories

One of the most critical aspects of growing your app after launch is **promotion**. While larger companies can afford expensive marketing campaigns, you can still achieve significant growth even with a limited budget.

The key is to use the resources available to you and to tap into free promotional channels that can generate awareness and drive downloads.

Social Media Marketing is one of the most powerful and cost-effective tools available. Platforms like Facebook, Instagram, Twitter, and TikTok provide immense exposure, and you can tailor your strategy to fit the platform's unique characteristics.

Start by creating a **content calendar** for your social media posts, showcasing your app's features, sharing success stories, and engaging with your users. Posting relevant content like tips, updates, or fun behind-the-scenes details can build an emotional connection with your audience. Don't forget to incorporate hashtags to increase discoverability, and encourage your users to share their experiences and reviews.

Another valuable tool is **free PR**. While press releases often come with a cost, there are many free services available that can help you gain media attention. Reach out to bloggers, journalists, and influencers in your niche. Share your app's story, explaining how it solves a real-world problem, its unique features, or your personal journey as an app creator.

Platforms like **HARO (Help a Reporter Out)** connect journalists with sources, offering opportunities for you to get press coverage for free. Even local publications or niche websites might be interested in featuring your app, especially if it addresses a specific need or fills a gap in the market.

App Directories are another often overlooked but powerful way to increase visibility. Websites like ProductHunt, BetaList, or AppAdvice allow you to submit your app and gain exposure to an audience interested in discovering new apps.

These directories are often visited by early adopters who are looking for fresh, useful apps. To make the most out of these platforms, ensure your app's listing is engaging, complete with screenshots, videos, and a compelling description.

While paid advertising options like Facebook Ads and Google Ads can also be beneficial, focusing on organic growth methods in the beginning stages of your app's lifecycle can save you money and help you build a loyal user base.

Building an engaged community around your app is one of the most sustainable growth strategies.

10.2 Updating and Maintaining Your App: Keep Your App Relevant and Bug-Free

Once your app is live, your job isn't over. In fact, the ongoing maintenance and improvement of your app are just as important, if not more so, than the development process. Regular updates not only improve the user experience but also help maintain relevance in a constantly changing digital landscape.

Bug fixes and performance enhancements are the most immediate areas to address post-launch. No app is perfect, and your users will inevitably encounter issues. It's essential to have a system in place to collect feedback from users and identify any bugs or glitches. Regularly monitoring app reviews and paying attention to user comments will allow you to spot any recurring problems.

Additionally, some no-code platforms offer tools to test your app in different environments, which can help identify bugs before they become widespread. Timely bug fixes are crucial for maintaining your app's reputation, and users are far more likely to trust an app that consistently works without crashes or errors.

Feature enhancements should also be part of your ongoing update strategy. As your app grows in popularity, new trends and technologies will emerge. Regularly updating your app by adding new features or improving existing ones helps keep the app exciting for current users while attracting new ones.

For example, you can introduce new themes, integration with other apps, or add in-app functionalities like notifications, messaging, or social media sharing. Additionally, don't hesitate to conduct A/B testing with new features to gauge user response before rolling them out to all users.

Compatibility with the latest devices and operating systems is another key reason why updates are essential. Both Android and iOS release new versions of their operating systems regularly, and apps must be compatible with these updates.

If your app isn't optimized for the latest iOS or Android version, it could lead to a poor user experience or, in the worst case, app crashes. Staying up-to-date with these system requirements is crucial for maintaining your app's functionality and ensuring that it's always available to users.

To ensure smooth communication with your users, make sure to inform them about the updates. A simple **update log** or changelog can be shared through app store descriptions or within the app itself. Let your users know what's new, whether it's bug fixes, a new feature, or general improvements. Keeping users informed shows that you are actively working to improve the app, which builds trust and loyalty.

Lastly, **user engagement** through updates is crucial. Encourage feedback after each update to understand whether the changes were well-received. You can use in-app surveys or email newsletters to solicit opinions and suggestions for further improvements.

Actively listening to users and implementing their feedback will build a strong, engaged community around your app.

10.3 Exploring Monetization and Scaling: Ads, Subscriptions, and Ideas for Your Next App

After launching your app and gaining users, it's time to think about how to generate revenue. Monetizing your app allows you to create a sustainable income stream while continuing to grow your business.

There are several approaches to monetization, and the choice depends on your app's type, audience, and goals.

In-app ads are one of the most common monetization strategies, especially for apps that are free to download. Platforms like Google AdMob or Facebook Audience Network make it easy to integrate ads into your app without requiring extensive development. There are various ad formats, including banners, interstitial ads, and rewarded video ads.

However, while ads can generate revenue, they must be implemented carefully to avoid disrupting the user experience. Too many ads, or poorly placed ads, can frustrate users and lead to a higher uninstallation rate. Finding the right balance between ads and usability is key to successful monetization.

Another popular option is **in-app purchases (IAP)**. This method allows users to download your app for free but offers premium features or content that they can purchase within the app. Whether it's unlocking advanced features, accessing additional content, or removing ads, IAP is an excellent way to monetize while still offering users value.

To succeed with in-app purchases, ensure that the free version of your app provides sufficient value to encourage users to upgrade, but also make the premium offerings enticing enough for users to spend money.

Subscriptions offer a more predictable revenue stream compared to one-time purchases. Subscription models are ideal for apps that provide continuous value, such as news apps, fitness apps, or productivity tools.

Offering tiered subscription levels can cater to different types of users, whether they want basic access or more advanced features. Subscriptions also offer the opportunity for ongoing engagement with users, as you'll need to provide new and valuable content regularly to retain subscribers.

If you're looking to scale your app, consider integrating **third-party APIs** or **partnerships**. APIs can enhance your app's functionality by integrating with other platforms, services, or tools.

For example, if you have a fitness app, you might integrate with fitness tracking devices like Fitbit or Apple Health. Partnerships with other brands or apps can also open up new revenue streams and expand your app's reach.

Lastly, as your app grows, you may want to explore creating **additional apps** to diversify your portfolio. With the knowledge and experience gained from your first app, you can identify other gaps in the market and create new apps to meet those needs.

Don't be afraid to experiment with different app ideas and business models. Your first app can serve as the foundation for a growing app ecosystem.

CONCLUSION

As we arrive at the conclusion of this book, it's important to reflect on the transformative journey you've undertaken—from nurturing an initial idea to bringing a fully functional mobile app to life using no-code tools. What once seemed daunting or reserved for professional developers is now within your reach, powered by your creativity, persistence, and the remarkable accessibility of modern no-code platforms. You've learned that building an app is not just a technical process—it's an act of problem-solving, storytelling, and connection.

Throughout this guide, we've demystified each step of the app-building process. You began by planning like a pro, laying a strong foundation through thoughtful feature prioritization, user flow design, and MVP development.

You then brought your vision to life visually, learning the fundamentals of mobile design, wireframing, and choosing an aesthetic that speaks to your app's identity. Armed with this visual clarity, you explored the wide world of no-code platforms and learned how to choose the right tool for your unique goals.

From there, you dove into the building blocks of your app—constructing screens, setting up navigation, and ensuring a user-friendly layout. You layered in core functionality: user input, dynamic content, media integration, and interactivity. You learned how to connect your app to a backend, how to manage and manipulate data, and how to structure everything using no-code logic to ensure a smooth and scalable experience.

But building doesn't end with development. You discovered how to test thoroughly, gather feedback, and iterate for constant improvement. You learned what it takes to prepare for launch, from app store compliance to live deployment, and finally, how to grow beyond launch—through marketing on a budget, keeping your app updated, and generating revenue with smart monetization strategies.

This book is more than just a manual. It's a blueprint for empowerment. You now possess the knowledge to turn ideas into reality, to innovate without code, and to think like a product creator—confidently, resourcefully, and strategically.

Whether this is your first app or one of many, you are part of a new wave of creators redefining what's possible in tech. You've proven that with the right tools and guidance, anyone can build something meaningful—no computer science degree required.

As you move forward, keep in mind that app development is never static. Markets evolve, user expectations shift, and technology advances. The beauty of the no-code movement is that it grows with you. Stay curious. Keep learning. Continue experimenting. Most importantly, keep building.

Let this be the beginning of a lifelong journey of creativity and innovation. Your first app is just the start. The next big idea is already forming—and now, you have the power to bring it to life.